How to Find a
Bra That Fits

HOW TO FIND A BRA THAT FITS

LIZ KUBA

Copyright © 2014 Elizabeth Kuba

All rights reserved.

ISBN: 1502793822
ISBN-13: 978-1502793829

Acknowledgements

Many thanks to Michael, Melissa, Caitlin, Maggie, /r/abrathatfits, and /u/mywifesbusty. Your help and knowledge has truly been invaluable.

CONTENTS

The Current State of the American Bra Industry 1

The Anatomy of a Bra 5

Naming Conventions and Sister Sizes 12

You Are Wearing the Wrong Size 17

Finding Your New Bra Size 19

Trying on Bras 23

Bra Care 28

Bra Myths 30

Does Wearing a Bra Put You at Increased Risk for Breast Cancer? 36

Fit Issues, Revisited 40

Closing Thoughts 46

Appendix A: Converting Between UK, US, European, and Australian Sizing 47

Appendix B: Sister Sizes and Cup Volumes 49

Appendix C: List of Places to Buy Bras 51

Appendix D: Resources 53

Glossary 55

About the Author 59

1
The Current State of the American Bra Industry

If you were born in the last several decades in America, you probably all went through the same rite of passage: you're going through puberty, and you finally hit that point where you need a bra. You've mustered up the courage to say something to your mom, who in all likelihood did one of a few things:

1. She went out and bought you the same size bra she wears.
2. She gave you one of her old bras.
3. She took you to Victoria's Secret, Aerie, or Dillard's to get fitted.
4. She took you to Wal-Mart/Target and left you to your own devices.

Then, for the next five/ten/twenty/forty years, you hated your bras. You constantly adjusted them throughout the day, ripping them off as soon as you got home. You knew it was time to buy a new bra when the old one finally broke, most likely because the wire started poking out.

And whenever you looked at yourself in the mirror, you looked at your chest and hated yourself.

You thought to yourself, if only your breasts weren't so small/large/weird/ugly/saggy/uneven, they'd look good in the bras. If only you lost some weight, or got a boob job, or worked out, or ate less, then you'd look like the models on the walls of the store, whose bras fit them perfectly. But since you're not that pretty and never will be, you'll just have to suck it up - because that's what you do with bras, you suck it up. It's part of being a woman, just like suffering through periods.[1]

Does that sound familiar? I sincerely hope not. If none of that sounds familiar, congratulations! This book probably isn't aimed at you (though you may learn a thing or two).

Most likely, though, some or all of this resonates with you. And I'm so, so sorry. It doesn't have to be this way, but it is. Don't blame your mom, she didn't know better. And don't even blame the fitters at the stores, because they didn't know better either.

American bra companies are to blame here. They've carefully cultivated the current state of bra fitting so that they can have as little innovation and as much profit margin as possible. That's what most other American companies do - is it so hard to believe that the bra industry would be any different?

--

---

[1] You don't actually have to suffer through periods, ladies. If your periods are making you (or the people around you) miserable, then please say something to your doctor. Chances are they can adjust some factors in your life, such as birth control, that can help smooth things out.

Let me introduce you to a concept I call The Bra Matrix. It's a grid of 25 bra sizes that most American companies say that everyone should fit in.

32A	32B	32C	32D	32DD
34A	34B	34C	34D	34DD
36A	36B	36C	36D	36DD
38A	38B	38C	38D	38DD
40A	40B	40C	40D	40DD

Table I. The Bra Matrix: 32–40 A–DD

That's it. These companies say that every single woman on this planet will most likely fit into those 25 sizes. There might be some outliers here and there (34AA, 38DDD, etc), but for the most part, that's it.

Betsey Johnson offers 20 sizes. Aerie offers 30 sizes. Victoria's Secret offers 40 sizes. Wacoal offers 55 sizes.[2] That doesn't sound too bad, right? I mean, 55 sizes is a *lot*.

The UK has several very large bra companies. One is Freya, and they offer roughly 85 sizes. Panache offers nearly 100 different sizes. Curvy Kate offers 105 sizes. Ewa Michalak, a Polish company, offers a whopping 120 sizes. So what gives? It's not like Americans are shaped more uniformly than the English or the Polish, so why are they so much more accommodating? Profit. Offering fewer sizes is so much cheaper, for several reasons:

Development costs: a 32A isn't just a shrunk down version of a 32D or a 38A. Every bra size is of a slightly different construction and shape. Developing a bra in 30 sizes is a lot quicker, cheaper, and easier than developing for 100 sizes.

Manufacturing costs: for the American companies, they only have to have 30 different templates per bra, as opposed to 80.

---

[2] Quantities are approximate and valid as of 2014.

Storage costs: keeping stock of 100 sizes per style is a lot more difficult and space-consuming than 30.

American bra manufacturers should be worried, though. Bra companies around the world are now available to us thanks to the internet. If Victoria's Secret and Aerie don't figure this out, they'll be swept by the wayside, because the average bra size is *not* 34DD.

2
The Anatomy of a Bra

For something that we wear every day, most of us understand very little about the bra. We don't even know what various parts of the bra are called. Quick, point at the gore! If you pointed at the fabric between the bra cups, congratulations, you know more about bras than most people.

To make sure everyone's on the same page, here's a diagram of your typical bra:

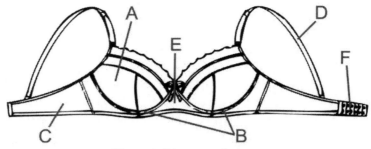

Figure 1. Diagram of a bra

A. Cups: Your breasts should be fully contained within this area.

B. Underwires: The underwire helps the bra keep its shape while being worn. Wireless bras aren't as supportive as wired bras, simply because they don't hold their shape as well. The underwires should always be sitting right in your inframammary fold (where the underside of your breast attaches to your chest).

C. Band: The band of the bra should be doing the majority of the work holding up your breasts. For most American bras, the band does not continue all the way around and beneath the cups, but rather is separated into sections: band, cup, gore, cup, band. For other bras, the band is one long strip of fabric (as shown in the diagram); the full-band style tends to be the sturdier of the two.

D. Straps: The straps should be doing very little of the work holding up your breasts. Some straps are fully adjustable (i.e., you can move the slider all the way from where it meets the band at the back to all the way at the front where it meets the cup). Some straps are only partially adjustable (i.e., there's only a limited amount that the straps can be adjusted).

E. Gore: The gore is the part of the bra where the cups meet at the middle. It should always be laying flat against your sternum.

F. Hooks: Most bras will have three columns of hooks, with two or three hooks in each column. If you start wearing the bra at the loosest hook and work your way to the tightest as the bra stretches out over time, more columns of hooks means your bras may last longer.

--

The cups themselves can vary greatly between bras. While each brand tends to describe the styles differently, the definitions below are the ones that I have found to be the most universal.

Padding amount

Unlined – the cup is simply mesh. If you lay the bra on a table, the cups completely collapse and the bra is flat. You will almost never see an unlined bra from an American bra company, but they are quite common outside of the US.

Lightly lined – the cups have a slight amount of padding. This is usually the thinnest bra that American companies will offer.

Lined/padded – the cups have a good amount of padding. Only the most persistent of nipples will show with a padded bra.

Push-up – the cups have a foam pad at the bottom and/or sides of the cup, pushing the breasts upwards (and sometimes inwards). Push-up bras are common in American brands, but fairly uncommon in bras made outside of the US.

Padding type

Unmoulded – The cups are soft and pliable, and will conform to the shape of your breasts.

Moulded – the cups have a rigid shape. If you can deform the cups at all, they will pop right back to their original shape as soon as you let go of the bra. Rather than conforming to your breasts, your breasts will be forced to take the shape of the bra. The vast majority of American bras are moulded, whereas very few bras outside of the US are moulded. As of 2014, 100% of the bras Aerie currently offers are moulded.

Shape

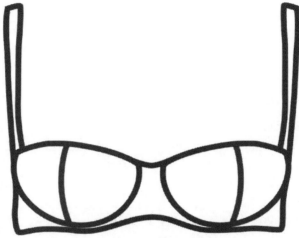

Figure 2. Half cup bra

Demi/half cup – the smallest amount of coverage. The top edge of the cup is close to parallel with the floor.

HOW TO FIND A BRA THAT FITS

Figure 3. Three-quarters cup bra

Balconette/three-quarters cup – an average amount of coverage. Also known as a balcony or balconet bra.

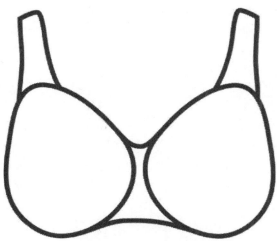

Figure 4. Full cup bra

Full cup – the breast is nearly fully encompassed by the bra cups; very little breast tissue is showing. Also called a full coverage bra.

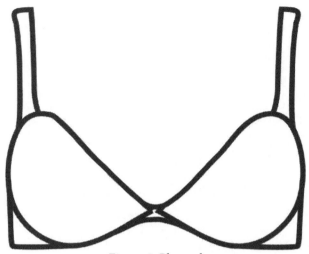

Figure 5. Plunge bra

Plunge – the gore is very short, made for plunging necklines. Nearly all of Victoria's Secret bras are plunge in shape.

Underwire presence

Underwire present – if the bra has no modifier, it almost always has an underwire.

Underwire not present – if the bra is lined and/or moulded and does not have a wire, it's usually called a *Wireless* bra. A wireless bra that is non-padded/unlined is usually called a *Bralette*. A wireless bra that is strapless is usually called a *Bandeau*.

--

HOW TO FIND A BRA THAT FITS

If you've only ever shopped at Aerie, Victoria's Secret, Dillard's, Target, etc, you may be wholly confused. It's quite understandable: American companies just call bras whatever they want. For example, Victoria's Secret is currently offering what they call an "Unlined Demi Bra." Most other companies around the world would call it a "Moulded Balconette Bra."

3
Naming Conventions and Sister Sizes

For me, the sizing system for bras used to make about as much sense as engine oil numbers. They seemed totally arbitrary and unintuitive. But, like engine oil weights, there is a method to this madness.

Every bra size is made up of two parts: a two-digit number (always even) and a letter (sometimes two). Each one means nothing without the other.

The number: for all modern bras, the number at the front of the size indicates the length of the band (the circumference). Specifically, the number is the length (in inches) of the band when it's stretched to its fullest. So, for an example, a 32 band bra will stretch out to 32" long (but will most likely be somewhere in the realm of 26"–30" when unstretched).

The letter: the letter corresponds to the difference between the fullest part of the bust and the band. Nothing more. A 2" difference corresponds to the letter B; an 8" difference corresponds to the letter FF. It is incorrect to say that someone is a [insert letter here]-cup.

The cup letter by itself does not mean anything. If someone says they're a C-cup, the only thing that can be logically inferred is that they have a 3" difference between their bust and their band. That's it. Full stop.

This means that cup size is not static. Although a 32B and a 40B both have 2" differences between the band and the bust, the actual cup volumes are different.[3]

Here's a representation of how breast volume changes with increasing cup sizes:

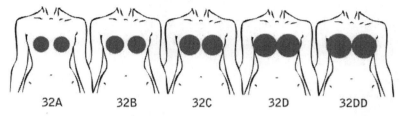

Figure 6. Five women with the same chest size, with different cup sizes; not to scale

That one is intuitive. Cup size goes up, breast size goes up.

To drive my previous point home (cup size is not static), the image below shows a representation of how breast volume changes with increasing band sizes. Even though all of these women wear a bra with a D cup, none of them have the same volume of breasts.

---

[3] Math interlude: Don't believe me? Think of it this way. A 32B is like having two circles, one of circumference 32" and another of 34". The difference in area between those two circles is $\frac{34^2}{4\pi} - \frac{32^2}{4\pi} = 92 - 81.5 = 10.5$ sq. in. Comparatively, the difference in areas for a 40B (42" and 40" circumferences) is 13.05 sq. in. So, logically, the cup volume of a 40B is larger than the cup volume of a 32B.

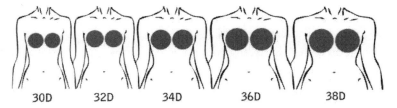

Figure 7. Five women with different size chests, with a 4" difference between their chest and bust measurement

Which brings me to my next topic: Sister Sizes. You may have heard this term bandied about by the associates at Victoria's Secret, but they never really seem to properly explain it. Two bras are sister sizes if the volumes of their respective cups are the same. But that doesn't really help at all, because bras don't come with their cup volume printed on the label.[4] So to put sister sizes in practice, when you go up a band size, you must go down a cup size.

Say you want to find a sister size of a 32D bra with a looser band (I'll explain why you would want this later). So if you want a bra with the same cup volume as a 32D but with a band size of 34, you'll want a 34C. Up one band size (32 to 34), down one cup size (D to C).

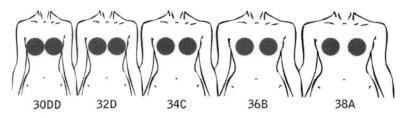

Figure 8. Five women with different chest sizes, but all have the same breast volume

---

[4] See Appendix B for a chart of bra sizes and cup volumes in cubic centimeters.

HOW TO FIND A BRA THAT FITS

These five bras all have the exact same cup volume: 30DD, 32D, 34C, 36B, 38A.

And these five bras are all the same volume: 28FF, 30F, 32E, 34DD, 36D.

These five are all the same volume, too: 36GG, 38G, 40FF, 42F, 44E.

A 30DD has the same size cups as a 38A. A 28FF will hold the same size breasts as a 36D. Someone whose breasts fit in a 36GG will find that their breasts are the same volume as someone whose breasts fit in a 44E.

Are you starting to understand why the cup letter is useless without the band size as well? I cringe every time I hear someone talk about "that chick with the double-D's." A 28DD has a very different volume than a 38DD. If you sister size 38DD down, you get 38DD, 36E, 34F, 32FF, 30G, 28GG (that is to say, a 38DD has the same volume as a 28GG). A 28GG bra holds much larger breasts than a 28DD bra. And then I think about how she's probably wearing the wrong size bra in the first place, and then I start wanting to yell at people. It's not a pretty sight.

The cup letter is useless without the band measurement.

--

I'd like to take a moment here to explain this naming convention. Here and throughout the book I use the sizing method known as the UK sizing method. I use this system because it is the most consistent and widely used method. For a chart on how to convert from UK to other naming conventions (European, Australian, and the various US ones), see Appendix A.

--

If you're handy with a needle and thread (or know someone who is), you can leverage sister sizes to your advantage. For example, if you wear a 28DD but like a bra that only comes in a 32 band, you can sister size up to a 32C and take the band in. If you only need to tighten the band by one size (e.g., you need a 26 but the bra only comes in 28 bands and above) and the band has exactly two or three hooks per column, a device called a Rixie Clip might be your savior (which can be found on Amazon or Etsy).

There's a solution for the opposite problem, too. If a bra doesn't come in a band size large enough for you, you can buy an extender. An extender acts as an extra set of hooks to lengthen your band by an inch or so. An extender can also be a life saver if you buy a new bra but the band is just a little too tight: the extender gives you some breathing room while the band stretches out over time. Once the band has stretched out a little, you can remove the extender and wear it like normal.

4
You Are Wearing the Wrong Size
(Or, How to Scoop and Swoop)

You are not wearing the right bra size.

I mean, of *course* you're not wearing the right bra size, 90% of women aren't. If your straps fall off, you're wearing the wrong bra size. If you have permanent dents in your shoulders from where your straps dig in, you're wearing the wrong bra size. If you're spilling out of the cups, if you constantly have back pain, if there's empty space in the cups, if you're afraid of flashing people when you lean over, you're wearing the wrong bra size. If you put on your bra by hooking it together *then* pulling it over your head and into place, you're definitely wearing the wrong bra size.

But even if you find your bra to be comfy, there's a good chance you're still wearing the wrong bra size. Let me prove it to you by teaching you something called the Scoop and Swoop.

Bra cups are meant to hold breasts, right? So in theory, a bra cup should contain the entirety of your breast tissue. The Scoop and Swoop is how you make sure all of your breast tissue is within the confines of the cup.

First, put on your bra however you normally do, and get it as comfortable as possible.

Lean over. Take your right hand and place it into your left bra cup. While still inside your bra, reach around to your side. Push into your side (Scoop) and pull all of your tissue towards the front and into the bra cup (Swoop). Repeat on the other side.

Now stand up. Oh goodness, that's a little indecent. Your nipples probably shouldn't be peeking out of the top of the cup, should they? Okay, okay, maybe it's not quite that bad, but there should be a smooth curve across your breast – there shouldn't be a valley at the edge of the bra cup (quadboob).

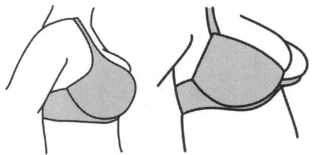

Figure 9. Quadboob, as viewed in profile (left) and three-quarters angle (right)

Now hop around a bit and jiggle yourself. Let your breasts settle into the cup however they want to. Did they go back to how they normally look? If so, that's another sign that you're not wearing the right size (your breasts shouldn't settle too much over the course of the day).

The ideal bra is one that you forget about once you put it on. If your bra does not meet that single criterion, then you're wearing the wrong bra size.

5
Finding Your New Bra Size

There are exactly three numbers that are going to change your life. And to get them, you only need two things: a close friend or family member, and a flexible measuring tape (like the kind tailors use). Please use inches for the purpose of finding your new size.

Step 0: Take everything you know about bras and bra sizing, and throw it out the window. It does not exist. You are a blank piece of paper, ready to absorb new inputs.

Step 1: Take off your shirt and bra. No, this is not optional. Yes, you will get a different (and wrong) bra size if you don't take off your bra. So take off your shirt and bra, stand up straight (don't slouch), and put your hands at your side.

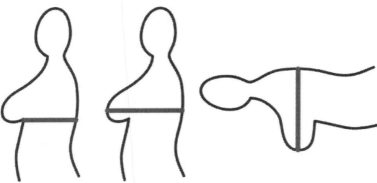

Figure 10. From left to right: chest (underbust) measurement, standing bust measurement, leaning bust measurement

Step 2: Measure your chest size. Have your friend measure the circumference of your ribs at the root of your breast (you may need to lift your breasts to allow the tape to go all the way up). Make sure the tape measure is snug up against the inframammary fold. Your friend needs to confirm that the measuring tape is exactly parallel to the ground. The measuring tape should be fairly snug, not loose. If the tape slips when you exhale, make it a little snugger.

Step 3: Measure your standing bust size. Have your friend measure the circumference of your torso at the fullest part of your breast. For most (not all) people, this will be at your nipple. Again, make sure the measuring tape is parallel to the ground. This time, though, do not pull the tape tight.

Step 4: Measure your leaning bust size. Lean over so that your back is now parallel to the ground and your breasts should be hanging freely, but keep your hands at your side. Have your friend measure the circumference at the fullest part of your breast, and make sure the measuring tape is exactly perpendicular to the ground. This number will be the same as or larger than the standing bust measurement. If this one is smaller than the previous, then re-measure both.

HOW TO FIND A BRA THAT FITS

Step 5: Calculate your band size. Your band size is the number you got from Step 2. If it's an odd number, round down (unless you have very little fat or need a looser band, in which case, round up).

Step 6: Calculate your average bust measurement. Add the measurements from Steps 3 and 4, and divide the sum by two.

Step 7: Subtract your chest measurement from your average bust measurement (Step 6 minus Step 2). To clarify, you'll want to use your actual chest measurement, not your rounded band size from Step 5.

Step 8: Use the number you got in Step 7 to count your way up the bra alphabet. This is your cup size. If your average is not a whole number, consider the two whole numbers on either side of it.

Difference (in)	<1	1	2	3	4	5	6	7	8	9	10
UK Cup Letter	AA	A	B	C	D	DD	E	F	FF	G	GG

Difference (in)	11	12	13	14	15	16	17	18	19	20	21
UK Cup Letter	H	HH	J	JJ	K	KK	L	LL	M	MM	N

Table II. The relationship between bust difference (in inches) and UK cup size; EE, I, II are not used

Step 9: Put together the band size you measured in Step 5 and the cup size you determined in Step 8. That's your shiny new bra size.

--

Confused? Me too. Let's use some examples. Here's some possible measurements for an imaginary lady. Let's call her Jill.

- Chest measurement: 33"
- Standing bust measurement: 39"
- Leaning bust measurement: 42"

Since Jill measured 33" underneath her breasts, we round down to find a band size of 32.

Next, we'll take the average of the two bust measurements; in this case, it's 40.5".

Take the difference to find the cup size: 40.5" - 33" = 7.5"

Count up the bra alphabet 7 and 8 steps: A, B, C, D, DD, E, F (7"), FF (8").

Jill's new bra size is either 32F or 32FF.

--

Now go measure yourself, and calculate your new bra size.

--

At this point, you're probably saying "Ha, 32G, are you crazy? I don't have porn star boobs, that's ridiculous." Or maybe "28D, that's stupid. I'm tiny, I'm pretty much flat-chested, the thought of having D cups is absurd."

Stop. Just stop right there.

I told you to forget everything you knew about bra sizing. Did you? No. That's okay. We've all been told since birth that AA = flat, A = tiny, B = average, C = a bit large, D = large, DD = very large, DDD... = porn star. I can't expect you to shed all of that indoctrination in the time it took you to read this chapter and measure yourself. But for now, I need you to just trust me. Write down your shiny new bra size (as well as its US equivalent, which can be found in Appendix A) and let's go to the bra store.

6
Trying on Bras

You've got your new size(s) in hand. Now what?

If this is your first time shopping for bras with your new size, I recommend going to a brick and mortar store to try things on in person. Nordstrom will be your best bet – they have a wide range of sizes and brands, and their associates have been trained using the sizing method outlined in this book. They're nearly universally kind and helpful, and will even offer alterations.

Not all of us are so lucky to have a Nordstrom nearby (and not all of us can afford Nordstrom prices). Some of us despise interacting with store associates. I will outline here how to shop for and try on bras by yourself.

First, you have to find a place. If you're lucky enough to fit in the Bra Matrix, Victoria's Secret and Aerie are available to you (just don't let their associates measure you). You also have stores like Wal-Mart and Target that you can browse through.

For those of us that don't fit within the bra matrix, we've got a limited number of options.

- Nordstrom – nice but pricey
- Nordstrom Rack – good prices but the selection is unpredictable
- Dillard's – not all stores offer sizes past DD, and very few offer sizes past FF
- Your local specialty boutique (see Appendix D) – will usually be pricey, but this is the only place you may find 28 band bras

Since this is your first time shopping, you'll want to do the shotgun approach. Grab as many bras as possible in the size(s) you calculated. Don't be afraid to go up or down a cup size or band size. We're just trying to actually confirm your new bra size.

Go to the fitting room and start trying bras on, following this procedure with each bra:

1. Loosen the straps
2. With the bra unhooked, put your arms through the straps
3. Hook the back of the bra to the loosest hook[5]
4. Scoop and swoop
5. Tighten the straps

When evaluating a bra for fit, here are some things to look for:

- You can only fit two or three fingers in between the band and your body.

---

[5] Not everyone is flexible enough to hook their bra together while it's on. If that sounds like you, hook your bra on backwards, spin it around, then put your arms through the straps and hike it up. This will be much more difficult with your proper band size than what you're used to.

- The straps stay up and don't dig in.
- There is a smooth curve along your breast, there's no quadboob.
- There's no wrinkling anywhere.
- The gore is flat against your sternum.
- Most importantly, the bra is comfortable.

You might start noticing that all the bras keep having the same problem, and that's a good thing! That will give you more clues on how to home into your proper size. Here's some common issues and how to fix them[6]:

- **Bra straps keep slipping off** – try sister sizing down to a smaller band size.
- **Bra straps are digging in** – try sister sizing down to a smaller band size.
- **Band is riding up in the back** – try sister sizing down to a smaller band size.
- **Band seems uncomfortably tight** – try putting the bra on backwards (so the cups are at your back. If it still feels too tight, then try sister sizing up to a looser band. If the band feels good when your breasts are not in the cups, go up a cup size or two.
- **Breasts are spilling out of the cup (quadboob appears)** – try going up a cup size.
- **Cups are wrinkling** – try going down a cup size.
- **The gore is not tacking (laying flat against the

---

[6] In each of these cases, the bra you're trying on just might be incompatible with you, and that's very common. If you've tried on several sizes of the same bra and they all have problems, just move on to the next one. See the Chapter 10 (Fit Issues, Revisited) for more information.

sternum)[7] – try going up a cup size.

Example 1: Jessica has tried on several 32B bras. The cups look good (no spillage or gaping), but the straps keep falling off. Jessica's next step would be to go down a sister size and start trying on 30C bras.

Example 2: Sam has found that every bra she's tried on in her new size of 28FF seems uncomfortably tight, and it seems impossible that she should be wearing a band that small. Before going up a band size, Samantha should double check that it's the band that's actually the problem. She decides to try on her bra backwards - this way, her breasts are no longer interfering and solely the band is being evaluated. When she tries it on backwards, the band feels really good, nice and secure but not too tight. Samantha's next step would be to try on some 28G and 28GG bras.

Example 3: Jordan calculated her size to be 34E, but it doesn't seem quite right. She's still spilling out of the cups and the bands keep riding up. In this example, Jordan has a combination of two different fit issues, and both need to be addressed. To compensate for spilling out of the cups, she'd go from 34E to 34F; and then to compensate for the band riding up, she'd sister size from 34F down to 32FF.

Example 4: Fatima calculated her bra size to be 38H, and from trying on bras that her size is indeed 38H. She tried on a bra in 38H, found that the cups were wrinkling, and went down a cup size to 38GG. The 38GG fit perfectly, even though there were other bras from the same brand that fit well in 38H. So which is her size, 38GG or 38H? Both! Fatima's a great example of how a single size isn't the end-all be-all of bra fitting.

---

[7] *Pectus excavatum* is a common congenital deformity in which the sternum looks caved in. If you have some degree of *pectus excavatum*, you'll have to rely on fit cues other than the gore.

Example 5: Keisha has tried on several 30F bras, but the straps keep digging in and her breasts keep drooping a bit. Her next step should be to sister size down and try on some 28FF bras.

--

The best bra is one that feels good to you. That being said, the first bras you try on in your new size will seem very firm and maybe even uncomfortable. You'll have to get used to a bra actually doing what it's designed to do: keep your breasts in place. However, there's a few things that won't just start to feel better over time, such as wires that dig in. If the gore is pressing into your sternum painfully, this may not be the bra for you.

Side note: If an associate has been helping you through the bra fitting process, it is generally considered good etiquette to buy at least one bra while you're there, particularly for local boutiques.

7
Bra Care

You've got your wonderful new bras, and you want to make them last as long as possible. There are only two rules for cleaning your bras:

1. Hand-wash using a gentle lingerie/delicates soap.
2. Never put the bras in the dryer.

Washing: Some brands of soap that are generally recommended are Soak, Eucalan, Forever New, Orvus Quilt Soap, and The Laundress Delicate Wash. I use Forever New because currently it's the most cost efficient. Follow the manufacturer's directions for washing, but make sure to be very gentle to the bras when releasing the extra water. Woolite is *not* a good soap for bras.

Drying: Do not wring your bras (especially moulded cups), but carefully roll them up in a towel. Nest moulded bras in each other so they don't get distorted when being rolled up. Hang your bras up (either on a clothesline or on plastic hangers) by the gore, not the straps. Never put your bras in the dryer.

There are a couple of guidelines for general care of your bras:

- Never wear the same bra two days in a row. This helps the elastic in the band "rest" between wears, rather than constantly being stretched out.
- Wash your bras every 2-3 wears. The more bras you own, the less often you'll have to have a washing party.
- When traveling, keep the back hooked together to prevent the hooks from damaging the body of the bra.
- Store moulded bras nested into each other to keep the cups from deforming.

Do you have to do this? Of course not. These are all just guidelines on how to get the most life out of your bra. Which leads me to my next point...

In general, a bra will only stay in good condition for roughly six months. You may get lucky and some of your bras may last much longer (especially if you have more bras in your closet that you rotate through). A good rule of thumb is when you've worked your way to the tightest hook and the band still feels a bit loose, it's probably time to retire it.

Oh, and never put your bras in the dryer.

8
Bra Myths

Myth: If my breasts weren't so weird, bras would fit better.
Reality: Your breasts are not weird. Your breasts are not weird. Your breasts are not weird. Say it with me, "My breasts are not weird." You are not fitting your breasts into the bra, you should be fitting a bra for your breasts. Your breasts are not weird or abnormal, they are beautiful and normal and wonderfully human.

Myth: My breasts are asymmetrical and there simply isn't a bra out there that'll work for me.
Reality: The majority of women have breasts that are not identical to each other. For most, the difference is one cup or less, but for many the difference is larger than one cup. In all cases, you should fit the bra to your larger breast. Simply tightening the strap slightly on the smaller breast can make the bra fit better for that breast. For women whose difference

is larger, the variation can be addressed by placing an insert (sometimes called a cookie or a cutlet) at the bottom of the cup of the smaller breast.

Myth: Once I find my bra size, every bra that comes in that size should fit.

Reality: All bras are created differently. They use different materials, different construction methods, and different cup shapes. Think of it like shopping for jeans – not all brands/lines of jeans will fit well.

Myth: Once I find my bra size, I only need to consider bras in that one size.

Reality: Again, like jeans, actual cup volumes will depend on the brand and line of bra. Just like how you may be a size 10 in one brand and a 14 in another, you can be a 36GG in one brand and a 34HH in another.

Myth: Once I find my bra size, I'm good for life.

Reality: Bodies change over time. You gain weight, you lose weight, you have a child, you breastfeed, you start a new method of birth control...any of these can have an effect on your breast size and shape. And sometimes breasts just change for no good reason at all. Consider re-measuring yourself at least once a year.

Myth: I should just go with whatever the store associate measures me as.

Reality: *Always* take what the store associate says with a grain of salt. Don't let them bully you into buying a bra you don't like. Don't be afraid to speak up (whether it's about asking them to bring you a bra in the size you measured yourself as or if it's about what you don't like about the bra they brought you), and don't be afraid to walk out.

Myth: The bra straps should be holding up my breasts.
Reality: The band of the bra, not the straps, should be doing 80% of the work.

Myth: I have large breasts, so I have to wear two bras when I exercise. One sports bra just doesn't cut it.
Reality: Sports bras are offered in the same range of sizes as all the other bras. Ones made by non-US brands are actually quite sturdy and there's a good chance you'll only need the one.

Myth: I have large breasts, so I'll always have back pain.
Reality: Wearing the proper size bra can reduce or even eliminate the back pain you experience due to having large breasts.

Myth: When trying on new bras, I should just hook the band on whichever hook is the most comfortable.
Reality: To get the most life out of your bras, you should be sizing and buying bras based on how the bra feels on the loosest hook. As your bra naturally stretches out over time, you move to a tighter hook to compensate for the loss in stretch. You're welcome to buy bras by how they feel on the tightest hook, but as the bra stretches out, there's nowhere to go. Caveat: if you love a bra but they don't make it in as small of a band as you need, you may be forced to wear it on the tightest hook from the beginning.

Myth: Nice bras and/or bras in "extended" sizes will cost a lot of money.
Reality: This depends on your definition of "a lot," but you can

spend as much or as little as you want on bras. Personally, my cheapest bra cost me $12, and my most expensive bra cost me $60. One of my favorite bras is one that I paid $45 for, on sale from $100. You can pay $10 for a secondhand bra on eBay, or you can pay $200 for a designer bra from Europe. You can pay $200 for a bra at a department store in America, or $15 for a new bra from a UK-based website. It's completely up to you. See Appendix C for more information.

Myth: Bras cause breast cancer.
Reality: Wearing a bra does not increase the risk of breast cancer. This is explained in the next chapter.

Myth: Wearing bras will prevent my breasts from sagging.
Reality: There is no evidence that wearing bras will prevent breasts from sagging over time.

Myth: Wearing bras will cause my breasts to sag.
Reality: There is no evidence that wearing bras will accelerate the natural sagging of breasts over time.

Myth: My breasts don't pass the "pencil test" (they can hold a pencil in place in the inframammary fold), so I must wear a bra.
Reality: Wearing a bra is a personal choice. The size and shape of your breasts should not be the sole factor in choosing whether or not to go braless.

Myth: I am not "officially a woman, with all the attendant glories" (per Ann Landers[8]) until I fail the "pencil test."

---

[8] West, Richard (June 1975). "Texas Monthly Reporter: Low Talk". *Texas Monthly* (Emmis Communications): 12. ISSN 0148-7736. Retrieved 2011-02-22.

Reality: Bullshit. If your gender identity is female, then you are a woman. End of discussion.

Myth: I am transgender, so I'm going to have a hard time finding bras that work for me.
Reality: I have found that transwomen fall into the American Bra Matrix more often than ciswomen. If that's the case for you, you'll actually have an easier time finding a bra that fits, simply because you have more options available to you. Please note that the method of bra sizing given in this book may overestimate your cup size a little.

Myth: Wearing a white bra is the best color bra to wear under a thin white shirt.
Reality: Wearing a bra that's close to your own skin tone will be much less visible than a white one. Most companies will have a bra that works for fairer-skinned women, but women with darker skin are sadly under-represented and will have a more difficult time finding a bra that matches their skin tone.

Myth: I shouldn't wear a bra with an underwire while breastfeeding.
Reality: It's okay to wear a bra with an underwire while you're breastfeeding, as long as you're confident that 100% of your breast tissue is within the cups. If your bra cups are too small and/or too narrow, the wire will be sitting on breast tissue, which inhibits the production of breast milk. That being said, you can find nursing bras in "extended" sizes.

Myth: If I take my bra off at the end of the day and I have red marks from it, I'm wearing too small of a band.
Reality: Red marks from a bra are very normal. They're just like the lines on your face from your pillow when you wake up, or

the lines on your calves from the top of your socks. If the lines stay visible for more than an hour, or you notice that the bra is rubbing sores into your chest, then your bra is too tight. (Caveat: if the red marks are itchy, painful, and present no matter what size band, then you may have an allergy of some kind. Go see a doctor.)

9
Does Wearing a Bra Put You at Increased Risk for Breast Cancer?

Short answer: No.

Long answer: This requires a bit of history to explain.

Enter Sydney Ross Singer and Soma Grismaijer. Singer has a BS in biology and a MS in cultural anthropology. Grismaijer has a BS in environmental studies and planning. The two are a husband-and-wife duo, and are self-proclaimed pioneers of applied medical anthropology.

In the 80s and 90s, the pair stayed very busy doing research on breast cancer, and in 1995 they published a book entitled *Dressed to Kill*. In this book, they purported that the reason bras increase the risk of breast cancer is due to the effect that bras have on the lymphatic system, particularly the circulation in lymph nodes. The constriction of a tight bra impedes the proper function of the lymphatic system, leading to a buildup of fluid within the breast tissue.

They claim that the lack of drainage is undesirable because this fluid is toxic: the substances that we take into our bodies via air, water, and food have all been polluted by petroleum and fossil fuels and are therefore carcinogenic. Consequently, when these toxins cannot flow normally through the lymph nodes, these toxins get concentrated in the breast tissue, leading to an increased risk of breast cancer.

Specifically, their findings were:

- 3 out of 4 women who wore their bras 24 hours per day developed breast cancer.
- 1 out of 7 women who wore bras more than 12 hour per day but not to bed developed breast cancer.
- 1 out of 152 women who wore their bras less than 12 hours per day got breast cancer.
- 1 out of 168 women who wore bras rarely or never acquired breast cancer.

They claimed that 70% of breast cancer cases were not explainable by the current (as of 1995) known breast cancer risks. They stated that breast cancer was a rare event in cultures that were bra-free.

Lastly, they blamed the green of the fashion and medical industries. The bra industry is a multi-billion dollar enterprise, and more billions of dollars are spent researching and treating the disease. Ironically, they note, ending breast cancer can cause financial hardship for many people.

Naturally, this book created quite a bit of discussion on the topic. Many medical and scientific bodies have studied and reviewed the authors' claims over that decade or so. In general, all of the authors' claims have been dismissed on the basis of poor methodology, lack of supporting evidence, and their failure to consider alternate explanations besides bra use for their findings.

Specifically, many researchers and scientists find the authors' claims to be unfounded for the following reasons (not an exhaustive list):

- Lack of controlled epidemiological data correlating bra-wearing with the risk for breast cancer
- Lack of proof that the pressure exerted by a bra reduces the flow of lymph
- Lack of proof that lymph contains carcinogens
- Lack of proof that there are carcinogens in the human body that can induce breast cancer
- Existence of published data correlating obesity with post-menopausal breast cancer
- None of the authors' surveys attempted to account for any of the well-known epidemiological risk factors for breast cancer, such as number of full-term pregnancies, age at first pregnancy, obesity, Western pattern diet, or use of medications such as hormone replacement therapy

In addition, the authors' theory about toxic fluid buildup in the lymphatic system was debunked by the National Institutes of Health. The NIH examined cancer rates among women who had their underarm lymph nodes removed as part of melanoma treatment:

> *"The surgery, which is known to block lymph drainage from breast tissue, did not detectably increase breast cancer rates, the study found, meaning that it is extremely unlikely that wearing a bra, which affects lymph flow minimally if at all, would do so."*[9]

---

[9] Ray, C. Claiborne (2010). "Q & A Bras and Cancer". *The New York Times*. Retrieved 2013-09-22.

The NIH[10], the American Cancer Society[11], and Breastcancer.org[12] all deny the link between bras and breast cancer.

So do bras cause breast cancer? No. Is there a link between not wearing a bra and lower rates of breast cancer? Perhaps. The authors of an NIH-funded study posit that, because of the known link between weight/obesity and breast cancer, women who have larger breasts are more likely to wear a bra than women with smaller breasts, and that bra cup size is often a reflection of weight.

Dressed to Kill is the sole reason some people think/believe that there's a link between breast cancer and wearing bras.

---

[10] "Breast Cancer." *Medline Plus*. National Institutes of Health. 30 Oct. 2013. Web. 10 Oct. 2014.
[11] "Appendix A: Breast Cancer." *American Cancer Society*. American Cancer Society. 21 Jun. 2014. Web. 10 Oct. 2014.
[12] "Can Wearing a Bra all the Time Cause Breast Cancer?" *Breastcancer.org*. Breastcancer.org. 17 Sep. 2012. Web. 10 Oct 2014.

10
Fit Issues, Revisited

The fit issues covered in the Trying on Bras chapter are the most common/universal fit issues, but you can really go down the rabbit hole on this topic. If you start reading this chapter and get really confused, then skip it and come back to it after you've tried on more bras.

Here I will explain the fit issues listed earlier in the book in greater detail.

Bra straps keep slipping off: sister size down to a smaller band.

Bra straps fall off the shoulders because the straps are set too wide. When the band is too large, the straps get too far away from the center of mass. Trying on a smaller band brings the straps back in closer to your spine.

Unfortunately, some bras are constructed so their straps are farther away from each other. If this is the case, no amount of sister sizing will bring the straps to a more stable position; you'll have to try a different bra.

Bra straps are digging in: sister size down to a smaller band.

If your straps are digging into your shoulders, it means that your straps are doing all the work in keeping your breasts up. As mentioned before, the *band* should be doing most of the work in keeping you supported, and a tighter band is more supportive than a loose band.

Band is riding up in the back: sister size down to a smaller band.

The band rides up in the back when your breasts don't have enough support. When they lack support, they sag. As the breasts slowly sag, the band (which is too loose to stay in place) rides up in the back to compensate. Again, a tighter band will give you the support you need.

Breasts are spilling out of the cups: go up a cup size.

When a bra cup is too small, all the scooping and swooping in the world won't make your breasts fit into a space that's too small. Keep going up cup sizes until you find that none of your breast tissue is escaping its confines.

Band seems uncomfortably tight: either go up a cup size or sister size up to a larger band, depending on the situation.

Many women are wearing bras with too small a cup volume. For them, sister sizing down feels impossible, as the band seems way too tight. What's going on here can be one of two things: either the band is just too small, or the cups are too small. When the cups are too small, breast tissue is forced out of the cup in any way possible, and one of the places it can go is down into the band area. This artificially increases your chest circumference, making the smaller band size feel suffocating.

For other people, though, it's a simple case of the band being too small. The easiest way to determine which category you fall under is to eliminate a variable: your breasts. The only way to evaluate the band alone is to try the bra on upside-down or backwards (so that your breasts are not in the cups). If the band still feels too tight, then you should sister size up to a larger band. However, if the band feels much better without your breasts in the cups, try going up a cup size or two.

Cups are wrinkling: either go down a cup size or the shape of the bra is wrong, depending on the situation.

The obvious answer here is that if you're not filling out the cup, the cup is too big. But for most people, going down a cup size doesn't eliminate the wrinkling completely. More often than not, it means that the bra you're trying on isn't the right shape for you. To make things more complicated, different kinds of wrinkling can indicate vastly different things about your breasts. The latter half of this chapter explains different breast shapes and all the different kinds of wrinkling they can cause.

The gore is not tacking: either go up a cup size or the shape of the bra is wrong, depending on the situation.

More often than not, a floating gore means that breast tissue is spilling out of your cups. Instead of the obvious quadboob, though, the gore not tacking indicates that the extra tissue is spilling out the bottom and/or insides of the cups. The breasts are being pushed together, so there's no room for the gore to go in between them and lay flat against your chest. Going up cup sizes moves the breast tissue back into the cups, creating space between the breasts.[13]

---

[13] To continue on this train of thought, your breasts will rarely create cleavage in a well-fitting bra. This might be a good thing for you: no more boob sweat! However, there are some times you just gotta have some

However, sometimes that particular bra has just too wide of a gore for you. Again, this is a breast shape issue, and you will learn more later in this chapter.

--

As mentioned before, though, not every bra will fit everyone. Breast shape can greatly affect how bras can fit. Outlined below are many different aspects of breast shapes and bra fitting that can be considered when trying on bras.

Breast Fullness Placement (a.k.a. FoT vs. FoB)

Description:

Full on Top (FoT) breasts are breasts that have the majority of their tissue on the top half of the breast. Full on Bottom (FoB) breasts are ones where the majority of the tissue is on the bottom half of the breast. If you're not sure which you are, one way to check is to lean over. If your nipples are pointed more forwards, you're probably full on bottom. If your nipples are pointed more backwards, you're probably full on top.

Fit issues:

If on most bras, the top edge of the cup seems to cut into your breast even when you're sure it's the right size, you may be FoT. Try bras that either are more open at the top of the cup (such as a half cup) or balconettes that have a stretchy top edge.

If the bras you're trying on keep gaping at the top edge, never

---

cleavage. One way to have cleavage but keep your breasts separate is to wear a bra with some push-up in the bottom but the top of the cups are parallel to the floor; this creates a Marie Antoinette effect. In addition, some plunges are specifically designed to push your breasts closer together, such as the Freya Deco Plunge. But in a pinch, you can always wear one of your old bras to get some cleavage when you need it.

laying flat/smooth across your breast, you may be FoB. Try balconettes that are more aggressively curved inwards at the top of the cup.

Breast Width (a.k.a. Narrow vs. Wide)

Description:
　　Wide breasts are ones whose root tends to wrap around the sides of the torso, sometimes even as far as reaching towards the back. Narrow breasts are ones where the outer edge of the root is at or in front of the arm pits. The hard part about addressing this issue is that no one particular bra style is generally wide or narrow. You just have to find bras by trial and error (or going online and searching).

Fit issues:
　　If the outer half of the underwire always feels like it's sitting on breast tissue no matter how much you scoop and swoop (and sizing up in the cup doesn't really help), you may have breasts with wide roots. Try wearing bras that have wider cups.
　　If it takes very little effort to scoop and swoop all your breast tissue into the cup, and there seems to be some empty space on the outside edges of the cups, you may have a narrow root. While this particular fit issue isn't necessarily a problem, if you find it uncomfortable, you may want to find bras with narrower cups.

Breast Depth (a.k.a. Shallow vs. Projected)

Description:
　　Unfortunately, this is a shape that you'll generally only figure out after trying on many bras. Women with projected breasts tend to have a smaller root and stick out from the body more.

Shallow breasts seem a lot smaller than they measure as, usually have a wide root, and are fairly flat. Women with breasts that measure at a D cup or less tend to have shallow breasts.

Fit issues:

If you can't ever seem to get the underwire directly up into your inframammary fold, or you often notice a crease/wrinkle in the cups just above the underwire, you may have projected breasts. Try looking for bras where the bottom edge of the cup is more perpendicular to the band.

If most bras, especially unlined ones, cut in at the top edge of the cup but seem way too big in the body of the cup (sometimes called orange-in-a-glass), you may have shallow breasts. Try demi cup bras and other bras that are very open at the top.

Breast Position (a.k.a. Wide-set vs. Close-set)

Description:

Wide-set breasts have a good amount of space between them, and two or more fingers fit easily between them. Close-set breasts are ones that have very little space between them, and it may be difficult to press even a single finger against the sternum without pressing on breast tissue.

Fit issues:

If the gore is always sitting on breast tissue, no matter what size cup you try on, you may have close-set breasts. Try bras with narrower gores, or try some plunges.

If there is usually a gap between the inside edge of the cup and the inside edge of your breast, you may have wide-set breasts. Try wearing a balconette bra and/or a moulded bra.

11
Closing Thoughts

A bra that fits well is quite possibly one of the most under-rated aspects of clothing. It gives us support, both literally and figuratively. It can affect our self-image and self-worth much more than we imagine. Bra fitting isn't an exact science, though. What works for one person may not work as well for another.

The bra fitting method outlined in Chapter 5 is simply a way to get *close* to your proper size. It's not the end-all be-all of bra fitting. That's why there's more text (Chapters 6 and 10) devoted to adapting this formula (as well as any other sizing formula) specifically for you.

Ultimately, the choice is yours. It's your body, your money, and your belongings. The best bra for you is the one that makes you feel good physically, mentally, and emotionally. I hope that the contents of this book bring you closer to that goal.

Appendix A: Converting Between UK, US, European, and Australian Sizing

Chest Measurement	UK	US	EUR	AU
26"	26	26	55	4
28"	28	28	60	6
30"	30	30	65	8
32"	32	32	70	10
34"	34	34	75	12
36"	36	36	80	14
38"	38	38	85	16
40"	40	40	90	18
42"	42	42	95	20
44"	44	44	100	22
46"	46	46	105	24
48"	48	48	110	26
50"	50	50	115	28

Table III. Approximate band size equivalents between various systems

Bust Difference	UK	US Common	US Cacique	US Le Mystere	EU	AU
<1"		AA				
1"	A	A		A	A	A
2"	B	B	B	B	B	B
3"	C	C	C	C	C	C
4"	D	D	D	D	D	D
5"	DD	DD	DD	DD/E	E	E
6"	E	DDD	DDD	F	F	F
7"	F	G	F	G	G	G
8"	FF	H	G	H	H	H
9"	G		H		I	I
10"	GG				J	J
11"	H				K	K
12"	HH				L	L
13"	J				M	M
14"	JJ				N	N
15"	K				O	O

Table IV. Approximate cup size equivalents between various systems (deviations may occur with various brands)

Appendix B: Sister Sizes and Cup Volumes

Bust Difference	1"	2"	3"	4"	5"	6"	7"	8"	9"	10"	11"
180	30A	28B	26C								
240	32A	30B	28C	26D							
310	34A	32B	30C	28D	26DD						
390	36A	34B	32C	30D	28DD	26E					
480	38A	36B	34C	32D	30DD	28E	26F				
590	40A	38B	36C	34D	32DD	30E	28F	26FF			
710	42A	40B	38C	36D	34DD	32E	30F	28FF	26G		
850	44A	42B	40C	38D	36DD	34E	32F	30FF	28G	26GG	
1000	46A	44B	42C	40D	38DD	36E	34F	32FF	30G	28GG	26H

Cup Volume (cc)

Table V. Sister sizes and cup volumes

Bust Difference	Cup Volume (cc)								
	1180	1370	1580	1810	2060	2340	2640	3000	3080
1"	48A	50A							
2"	46B	48B	50B						
3"	44C	46C	48C	50C					
4"	42D	44D	46D	48D	50D				
5"	40DD	42DD	44DD	46DD	48DD	50DD			
6"	38E	40E	42E	44E	46E	48E	50E		
7"	36F	38F	40F	42F	44F	46F	48F	50F	
8"	34FF	36FF	38FF	40FF	42FF	44FF	46FF	48FF	50FF
9"	32G	34G	36G	38G	40G	42G	44G	46G	48G
10"	30GG	32GG	34GG	36GG	38GG	40GG	42GG	44GG	46GG
11"	28H	30H	32H	34H	36H	38H	40H	42H	44H

Table VI. Sister sizes and cup volumes, continued

Appendix C: List of Places to Buy Bras

Offline (brick and mortar) retailers:
- Aerie
- Bloomingdale's
- Dillard's
- Frederick's of Hollywood
- Intimacy
- JCPenney
- Kohl's
- La Perla
- Lane Bryant
- Nordstrom
- Sears
- Soma Intimates
- Victoria's Secret

Online retailers (aggregate):
- Amazon.com
- ASOS.com
- Butterflycollection.ca
- Brastop.com
- BreakoutBras.com
- Figleaves.com
- Hautelook.com
- Lulalu.com
- Net-a-porter.com
- Nordstrom.com
- Theoutnet.com
- Trueandco.com
- Wacoal-america.com

Zappos.com
Zulily.com

Online retailers (single company):
Avocado.com.pl
Bravissimo.com
Change.com
Comexim.pl
Damaris.co.uk
Ewa-michalak.pl
Store.myintimacy.com
Marksandspencer.com
Thelittlebracompany.com

Secondhand/cheap sources:
Bratabase.com
eBay.com
eBay.co.uk
Reddit.com/r/BraSwap
Reddit.com/r/RandomActsOfBras

Appendix D: Resources

The Busty Resources Wiki – http://bustyresources.wikia.com/
This Wiki is an incredibly comprehensive website that covers many topics with helpful pictures and videos.

List of Brick and Mortar stores –
http://bustyresources.wikia.com/wiki/Offline_retailer
This is a list of specialty boutiques, sorted by state. Even though it's perpetually a work in progress, it's a great place to start.

Bratabase – http://www.bratabase.com/
Women get together and enter in the measurements of all of their bras. When buying bras online, Bratabase is invaluable. By measuring the bras that fit you and comparing it to the information on the bra you're considering, you can get an idea of whether or not it may fit. They also have a comprehensive breast shapes gallery.

Reddit – http://www.reddit.com/r/abrathatfits
A wonderful group of people dedicated to helping people find that perfect bra. They offer personal fit solutions, as well as discussions over a range of topics.

Busenfreundinnen – http://busenfreundinnen.net/
A German-based website similar to Reddit, but in forum form. They offer a slightly different perspective than Reddit, but you will need to become friends with Google Translate.

007 Breasts – http://www.007b.com/breast_gallery.php
A website for showing pictures of normal women with no bras on (warning: explicit content). Your breasts are not weird!

The Bra Band Project – http://www.brabandproject.com/
A website dedicated to showing pictures of what women look like using the sizing method I give here in this book. It's a great way to convince you and your friends that you are indeed the size you measured yourself as.

Glossary

This glossary will contain words and phrases found both here in the book as well as terms not covered in the book but may be encountered in the course of bra shopping.

Balcony/Balconet/Balconette bra – see *three-quarters cup bra.*

Band – the stretchy strip of fabric on the bra that goes all the way around the torso and hooks at the back.

Bandeau bra – a strapless bra with no wire.

Bra – ~~a medieval torture device~~ an undergarment used to support a woman's breasts.

Bra matrix – the small range of sizes offered by most bra companies based in the US: 32-40 A-DD.

Bralette – an unlined wireless bra.

Ciswoman – someone that was assigned female at birth and identifies as a woman.

Cookie – see *insert.*

Cups – the part of the bra where one's breasts are wholly contained.

Cutlet – see *insert.*

Demi bra – see *half-cup bra.*

Extender – an extra set of hooks that can be attached between the two ends of the band of a bra, causing the band to be a bit longer.

Full cup bra – a bra designed to fully cover the entire breast. Also called a *full coverage bra.*

Full on bottom – breasts that have more mass on the bottom half than the top half.

Full on top – breasts that have more mass on the top half than the bottom half.

Gore – the bit of fabric at the middle of the bra between the two cups.

Half-cup bra – a bra with cups that are short and the top edge is close to parallel with the ground, designed to have very little coverage. Also called a *demi bra*.

Hooks – the hook-and-eye system that connects the back ends of the band.

Inframammary fold – the point at which the breast tissue attaches to the chest wall on the underside of the breast.

Insert – a small crescent of padding designed to be placed at the bottom of the cup of the bra. Sometimes used in both cups to turn a regular bra into a push-up bra; can be used in a single cup to help correct for breast asymmetry. Also called *cookie* or *cutlet*.

Lightly lined bra – a bra that has a very small amount of thickness to the cup walls.

Lined bra – a bra that has some padding in the cups. Also called a *padded bra*.

Longline bra – a bra with a band that is taller/longer than usual. Usually has three or more hooks per column at the back.

Moulded bra – a bra that has rigid cups that do not deform.

Multiway bra – a bra where the straps can be removed and re-attached in various ways in order to be better hidden under diverse shirts/dresses.

Nursing bra – a bra with cups that are flaps and can be folded down for the ease of breastfeeding.

Orange-in-a-glass – the effect created when too projected of a bra is placed on too shallow of a breast. Imagine setting an orange in a glass: the breast is the orange, and the bra is the glass.

Padded bra – a bra that has some padding in the cups. Also called a *lined bra*.

Plunge bra – a bra with a very short gore, designed to be worn under shirts/dresses with plunging necklines and not be seen.

Projected – breasts that stick out more than the average person.

Push-up bra – a bra that has a pad in the cups designed to put the breasts upward and/or inward, giving the effect of having larger breasts.

Quadboob – the effect when a bra is too small and the breast tissue is spilling out of the top of the cup, but the top edge of the cup is cutting into the breast. Also called *quadraboob* or *quadroboob*.

Racerback bra – a bra with straps that meet together at the middle of the back, rather than never meeting and attaching to the band at the sides.

Racerback converter – a device that brings the bra straps together at the back. Used to hide bras under racerback shirts and/or keep straps from falling down.

Rixie Clip – a device that attaches to the band of a bra that shortens the length of the band. Can be found on Amazon, Etsy, or RixieClip.com.

Scoop and swoop – the method by which all the breast tissue is moved into the cups of the bra. Also called the *scoop and grab* or the *scoop and jiggle*.

Shallow – breasts that have a wider base with very little projection.

Sports bra – a bra designed specifically for use during exercise.

Strapless bra – a bra that does not have any straps, designed to be worn with shirts/dresses with small/no straps. See also *bandeau bra*.

Straps – the strips of elastic that your arms go through and connect the front of the bra to the back of the bra, and are adjustable in length.

Tack – lay flat against the chest.

Three-quarters cup bra – a bra with a moderate amount of

coverage. Also known as a *balcony*, *balconet*, or *balconette bra*.

Transgender – someone whose gender identity does not match the gender they were assigned at birth.

Transwoman – someone who identifies as female but was not assigned female at birth.

Underwire – the U-shaped length of metal or plastic that sits along the bottom of the cup, designed to give the bra structure.

Unlined bra – a bra where the cups are completely mesh, with no lining or padding at all.

Unmoulded bra – a bra with cups that are not rigid.

Wireless bra – a bra that does not have an underwire. See also *bandeau bra* and *bralette*.

About the Author

Liz Kuba stumbled across her real bra size in 2010 and has never looked back. She tries to keep her bra-vangelizing to a minimum, but her enthusiasm sometimes gets the best of her. She likes racing cars and sewing clothes, and when the mood strikes her, she'll break out the French horn. Liz earned her Bachelor of Science in Ceramic Engineering at Missouri University of Science and Technology and currently resides in St. Louis, MO. She can be contacted at www.brathatfits.me.

Printed in Great Britain
by Amazon